WORLD FACT FILES

The Caribbean

Alison Hodge

MACDONALD YOUNG BOOKS

First published in 1998 by Macdonald Young Books
An imprint of Wayland Publishers Ltd
© Macdonald Young Books 1998

Macdonald Young Books
61 Western Road
Hove
East Sussex
BN3 1JD

Find Macdonald Young Books on the Internet at
http://www.wayland.co.uk

Design and typesetting Roger Kohn Designs
Commissioning Editor Hazel Songhurst
Editor Merle Thompson
Picture research Bridget Tily
Maps János Márffy

The Consultant, **Rob Bowden**, is a development geographer
at the University of Brighton. He specializes in developing areas
and has worked in, and taught on Africa, Asia and the Caribbean.
He has co-authored other geography books and is currently
working in Zimbabwe.

We are grateful to the following for permission to reproduce the
photographs, which were selected by the publishers:
Front Cover: Pictures, *above*;
Robert Harding, *below* (John Miller);
Allsport, page 25 (Shaun Botterill); Colorific/Telegraph, page 20
(Randa Bishop); Comstock Photo Library, pages 26, 33 (Mike
Andrews); Howard Davies, page 15; James Davis, page 34 *below*;
Eye Ubiquitous, pages 8 (Eric Enstone), 10 (Gavin Wickham),
31 (David Cumming), 34 *above* (Bruce Adams), 43 *above* (Lawson
Wood); Alison Hodge, pages 24 *above*, 41; Jeremy Horner, page
37 *below*; John & Penny Hubley, page 22 *above*; Hutchinson
Library, pages 14 (Philip Wolmuth), 16 (Philip Wolmuth), 18 (Sarah
Errington), 21 (J Henderson), 23 (N Durrell McKenna), 38
(S Errington); Impact, pages 29 *above* (Christopher Pillitz), 40
(Gary John Norman); Roger Kohn, page 43 *below*; Panos, pages
13 *below* (Marc French), 19 (Micheal J O'Brien), 22 *below* (Neil
Cooper), 29 *below* (Marc French), 30 *above* (Philip Wolmuth),
36 (Liba Taylor), 44 (Liba Taylor); Photographers International Ltd,
page 11 (Jayne Fincher); Pictures, pages 32, 37 *above*, 42; Still
Pictures, page 17 (Mark Edwards); Topham Picturepoint, page 24
below; Trip, pages 27 (R Belbin), 30 *below* (D Davis); Travel Ink,
pages 12 (Abbie Enock), 28 (Abbie Enock); Wayland, pages 9
(Howard Davies), 13 (*above*), 35, 39 *above* and *below*.

The statistics given in this book are the most up to date
available at the time of going to press

Printed in Hong Kong by Wing King Tong

A CIP catalogue record for this book is available from
the British Library

ISBN: 0 7500 2434 8

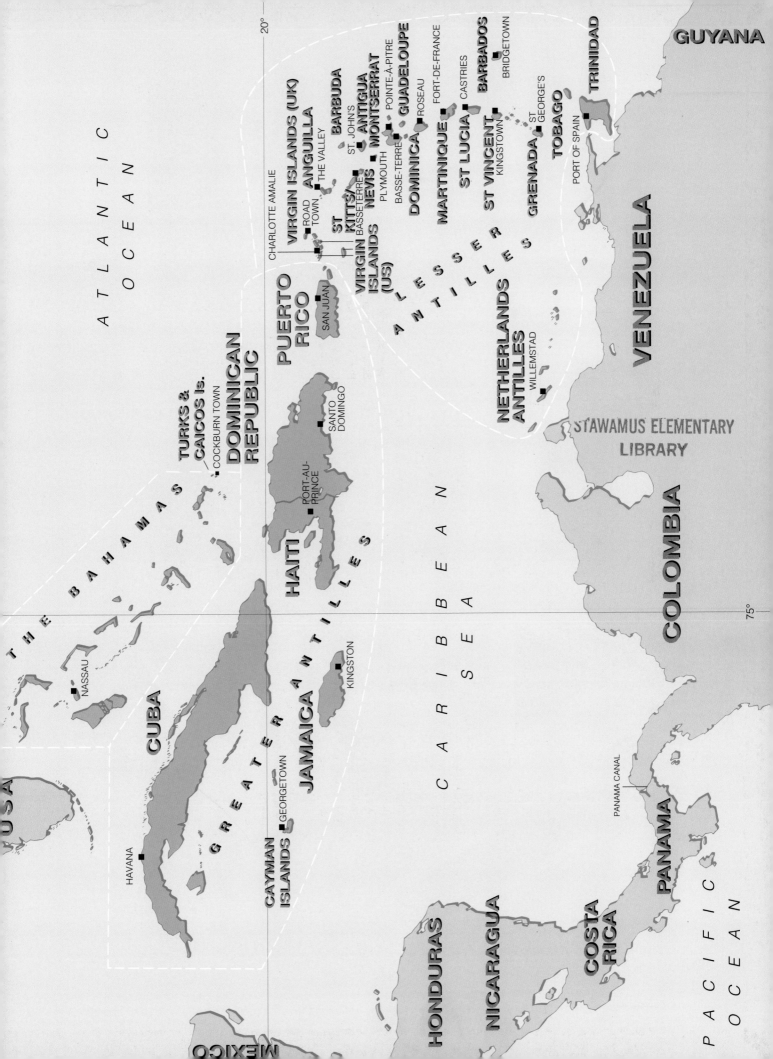

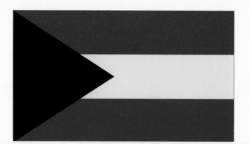

The Bahamas

Barbados

Cuba

Dominica

Dominican Republic

Guadeloupe

Haiti

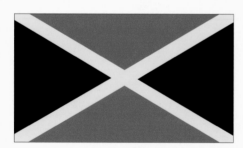

Jamaica

Puerto Rico

St Lucia

Trinidad and Tobago

US Virgin Islands

Words that are explained in the glossary are printed in
SMALL CAPITALS the first time they are mentioned in the text.

INTRODUCTION

The Caribbean islands, or the West Indies, as they are sometimes known, are made up of three separate groups of islands known as archipelagos. The largest, the Greater Antilles, includes Cuba, the Dominican Republic, Haiti, Jamaica, and Puerto Rico. The Lesser Antilles include Antigua, Dominica, Grenada, Trinidad and Tobago, and the Virgin Islands. The third archipelago, The Bahamas, has over 700 smaller islands, among which are Andros, New Providence, Grand Bahama and San Salvador. Together, the Caribbean islands cover a land area of approximately 238,371 square kilometres ranging from Cuba at 114,525 square kilometres to Anguilla at just 91 square kilometres. The islands take their name from the Caribbean Sea. This, in turn, is called after some of the earliest inhabitants of the region, the Carib people.

After they were discovered by the Genoese explorer, Christopher Columbus, in 1492, the Caribbean islands were colonized by Europeans. The British, Dutch, French and Spanish overcame the local Carib and Arawak people and struggled amongst themselves to gain control of the islands. They developed sugar plantations, creating a demand for

▼ *In Port of Spain, Trinidad, carnival bands parade for two days before Ash Wednesday. Some of the colourful costumes can be as tall as 4 metres.*

labour that was met by shipping in hundreds of thousands of slaves from West Africa. Since the 1950s, several of the islands have become independent, but many still have dependent relationships with their former colonial powers.

Today, the Caribbean has a colourful mix of cultures, people and lifestyles. Evidence of the region's long and dynamic history can

▼ *A statue of the musician Bob Marley who grew up in Trench Town – a poor part of Kingston, Jamaica. In the 1970s, he became an international superstar and made reggae popular throughout much of the world, especially in Europe and America.*

THE CARIBBEAN AT A GLANCE

● Population: 35.7 million (1996)
● Population density: An average of 150 people per square kilometre. Barbados has 598 people per square kilometre while The Bahamas has 19 people per square kilometre
● Largest cities: Havana (Cuba) 2.1 million, Santo Domingo (Dominican Republic) 2.2 million, Port au Prince (Haiti) 1.4 million, Kingston (Jamaica) 0.6 million
● Highest point: Pico Duarte in the Cordillera Central (Dominican Republic), 3,175 metres
● Official languages: English, Spanish, French, Dutch (on different islands)
● Religions: Christianity on all the islands, also Islam, Hinduism (Trinidad & Tobago), Rastafarianism (Jamaica), voodoo (Haiti) and other spiritual cults
● Major resources: BAUXITE, petroleum, nickel, salt (on different islands)
● Major products: sugar-cane, bananas, rum, coffee, spices, cocoa, citrus fruits, tobacco, clothing and textiles, electronic equipment, minerals, oil (on different islands)
● Environmental problems: soil erosion, DEFORESTATION, water scarcity (some islands)

be found in all areas of modern life. Many people think of the Caribbean as a place of tropical beaches, vibrant people, exotic fruits, and reggae music. There is another, less familiar, side to the Caribbean. Poverty is widespread and rapid population growth threatens the fragile environments and delicate economies of the islands. This book explores all aspects of the modern Caribbean and considers the likely trends and prospects for the region's future development.

THE LANDSCAPE

The Caribbean islands form a broken bridge of land, some 3,000 kilometres long, between Florida in the USA and Venezuela in South America. The islands separate the Atlantic Ocean from the Caribbean Sea, which covers an area of 1,943,000 square kilometres. It is rarely less than 1,830 metres deep, and where a fault in the earth's crust results in deep ocean trenches, depths of over 3,660 metres are common. This fault means that there are frequent earth tremors and occasionally large earthquakes. It is also the cause of the region's most spectacular feature – its volcanoes. The volcano on the island of Montserrat, Soufrière Hills, began erupting in July 1995, and shows how

▼ *The islands of the Greater Antilles are mountainous. Jamaica's Blue Mountains range from the northern suburbs of Kingston to the north coast, and reach a height of 2,256 metres.*

powerful the forces are that lie under the Caribbean. Many of the islands like the inner chain of the Lesser Antilles are, in fact, remnants of past volcanoes. This chain is part of a submerged, and still active, volcanic ridge.

The Greater Antilles are the exposed part of a submerged mountain range, once linked to mountains in Central and South America. Heights of 2,000–3,000 metres are common on the islands of Hispaniola (shared by the Dominican Republic and Haiti) and Jamaica, but the remainder of the islands are rarely higher than 1,500 metres.

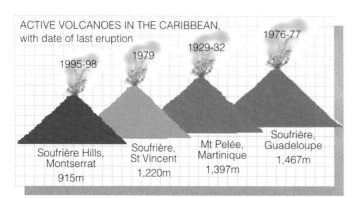

ACTIVE VOLCANOES IN THE CARIBBEAN, with date of last eruption

1995-98 Soufrière Hills, Montserrat 915m

1979 Soufrière, St Vincent 1,220m

1929-32 Mt Pelée, Martinique 1,397m

1976-77 Soufrière, Guadeloupe 1,467m

▲ *Soufrière Hills, one of seven active volcanoes on Montserrat, began erupting in July 1995, sending ash clouds up to 12 kilometres in the air and plunging much of the island into darkness. People living near the volcano have been evacuated.*

KEY FACTS

● The Caribbean Sea is approximately 3.5 times bigger than the North Sea off the UK, but only a sixth of the size of Hudson Bay, in Canada.

● At 7,353 metres, the Cayman Trench between Jamaica and the Cayman Islands is the deepest known point of the Caribbean Ocean. Milwaukee Depth, north of Puerto Rico in the Atlantic Ocean, is 9,200 metres deep.

● In 1692, an earthquake destroyed Port Royal on Jamaica and, in 1907, much of the capital, Kingston, was destroyed by another powerful quake.

● In 1902, Mount Pelée, on the island of Martinique, erupted killing 29,000 people – the greatest loss of life caused by a volcanic eruption in the 20th century.

Several of the smaller islands, such as those in The Bahamas, are extremely low-lying areas of limestone or coral. Sometimes they rise only 50–100 metres above sea level. Limestone is common throughout the region. In Cuba, Jamaica and Puerto Rico, it appears as spectacular TROPICAL KARST, known as 'cockpits' because of its appearance. The low-lying islands and limestone plains are often swampy, with mangroves and salt marshes in the coastal regions. In contrast, the more mountainous areas are clad with tropical forests and cascading waterfalls such as those around Ocho Rios in Jamaica.

CLIMATE AND WEATHER

Apart from The Bahamas, the Caribbean lies entirely within the TROPICS. The prevailing North East Trade Winds that cross the Atlantic from Europe and West Africa, moderate the tropical temperatures. This means that the islands have an equable tropical maritime climate.

Temperatures are relatively stable throughout the year, but vary between islands depending on their height above sea level and the effect of the cooling trade winds. In general, temperatures vary from around 18–28°C in January to 25–35°C in July except in the mountains and on the coast, where it is a few degrees cooler. Rainfall also varies between islands. Generally, there is a wet season from June to November, and a dry season between December and April. Mountainous areas, such as the Blue Mountains of Jamaica, receive more than 5,000 mm of rain per year. Low-lying islands, such as the Turks and Caicos, have an average of around 710 mm. Flash floods occur during the frequent thunderstorms of the rainy season.

Between July and October, the Caribbean

◀ *Cable Beach, on New Providence Island, in The Bahamas is a typical Caribbean white sand beach. Beaches such as this, and the warm sunny climate, are vital to the region's tourist industry.*

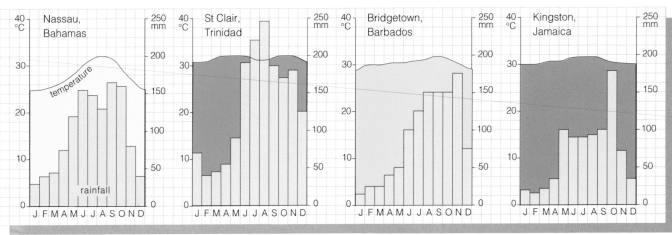

◀ *Storm clouds building over Havana, in Cuba. Thunderstorms are frequent in the rainy season and can often cause flash floods.*

▶ **Wrecked houses in Allman Town, Kingston, after Hurricane Gilbert struck Jamica in 1988.**

KEY FACTS

● In the Blue Mountains of Jamaica, rainfall can exceed 5,000 mm a year. Bowden Pen, in the Upper Rio Grande Valley, holds the Jamaican record with 12,598 mm in 1959/60.

● Strong winds and heavy rain are common during the hurricane season. Tropical storms occur when the wind speed is between 65–120 kilometres per hour. If the wind exceeds 120 kilometres an hour, the storm is classified as a hurricane.

● In November 1994, tropical storm Gordon swept across Haiti, causing flooding that killed at least 829 people and left over 10,000 homeless.

is at risk from one of the world's most feared natural hazards – hurricanes. These swirling winds of up to 300 kilometres per hour are formed over warm tropical seas and develop in the trade winds, sucking up water vapour to form towering storm clouds. As they hit land, they can devastate property and the environment, causing loss of life and severe economic damage. In 1988, Jamaica was hit by Hurricane Gilbert which, with winds gusting to 350 kilometres per hour, was the worst recorded hurricane of the century. In general, the Caribbean can expect at least one threatening hurricane every year.

NATURAL RESOURCES

The most striking thing about the natural resources in the Caribbean is their uneven distribution. Islands such as Jamaica, with its rich bauxite deposits, and Trinidad with its oil and gas reserves are in stark contrast to Antigua, Guadeloupe and Martinique, which have almost no mineral resources. Looking at the region as a whole, it has four significant minerals – bauxite, crude oil, nickel, and salt.

Salt is the only mineral that is widespread throughout the islands and, in the past, many of the islands had productive SALT PANS. Today, The Bahamas produces the largest amount of salt, around 700,000 tonnes per year. Cuba and the Netherlands Antilles also produce substantial quantities.

In 1980, the Dominican Republic, Haiti and Jamaica all produced significant quantities of bauxite but, by the 1990s, declining world prices forced all but the Jamaican mines to close. In 1994, Jamaica was the world's third biggest producer of bauxite and the mineral accounted for over half of the country's export earnings.

Cuba and the Dominican Republic are important producers of nickel and nickel ore. These are used in the production of

▲ **Trinidad has a Pitch Lake that produces asphalt, the material used to pave most of the world's roads. The lake, which is said to be a million years old, covers around 40 hectares and is up to 90 metres deep in the centre.**

KEY FACTS

● The northern coast of the Dominican Republic is called the Amber Coast, because some of the most beautiful amber in the world is mined here.
● After Australia and Guinea, Jamaica was the world's biggest producer of bauxite in 1994, producing 9,625 tonnes, or approximately 9.5% of total world production.
● A US$ 1,000 million liquefied natural gas plant at La Brea, in Trinidad, is one of the Caribbean's largest investment projects, and will produce electricity for the island's inhabitants.
● Oil was first extracted in Trinidad and Tobago from onshore oilfields in 1876, making it one of the world's oldest sources.

metal alloys and plated steel. In 1993, Cuba produced 30,000 tonnes of nickel ore and the Dominican Republic 24,000 tonnes.

Crude oil is found in Barbados, Cuba and Trinidad, but only Trinidad has significant reserves. When offshore extraction began in 1969, Trinidad's economy boomed and people prospered, with the GROSS NATIONAL PRODUCT (GNP) PER CAPITA rising to US$ 6,600 by 1982. However, falling oil prices in the 1980s meant that, by 1994, income per capita had fallen to about US$ 3,700. Today, oil reserves are becoming exhausted and, in the 21st century, natural gas is expected to replace oil as Trinidad's main export resource.

Extracting minerals is an expensive and risky process for any economy, but especially for developing economies like those of the Caribbean. Because of the costs, foreign MULTINATIONALS undertake much of the work but this means that a large proportion of the profits goes to those countries and does not stay in the Caribbean. In the 1970s, the Jamaican government recognized this problem. It

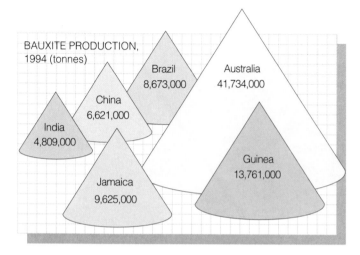

BAUXITE PRODUCTION, 1994 (tonnes)

India 4,809,000

China 6,621,000

Brazil 8,673,000

Australia 41,734,000

Jamaica 9,625,000

Guinea 13,761,000

◀ *Bauxite, Jamaica's 'red gold', is found in the hollows of limestone rocks in the highlands. It is extracted by open-cast mining, using huge excavators and trucks like this one driven by a woman worker.*

bought shares in the island's bauxite companies and imposed taxes on production. In this way, it was able to increase the country's share of the bauxite revenue. But such measures do not always protect the economy, because the price of minerals often fluctuates on the international markets. This causes problems for those islands which rely heavily on one or two mineral commodities.

Besides minerals, the Caribbean's main natural resource is its land and climate. The land is used to grow crops for export, and the tropical climate and beautiful scenery are the centre of a thriving tourist industry.

ENERGY

The Caribbean has few energy resources and relies heavily on imported petroleum products. Some islands, such as Trinidad and Tobago, can supply their own needs, and a new natural gas plant at La Brea should ensure future supplies. Other

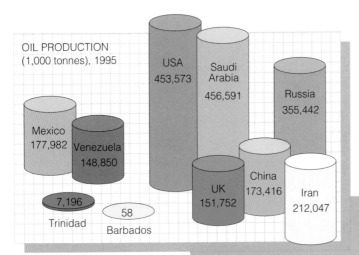

OIL PRODUCTION
(1,000 tonnes), 1995

USA 453,573
Saudi Arabia 456,591
Russia 355,442
Mexico 177,982
Venezuela 148,850
UK 151,752
China 173,416
Iran 212,047
7,196 Trinidad
58 Barbados

▶ *An oil platform at Galeota Point, south-east Trinidad. Oil was first extracted from the ocean bed around Trinidad in 1969, and this led to an economic boom in the country throughout the 1970s.*

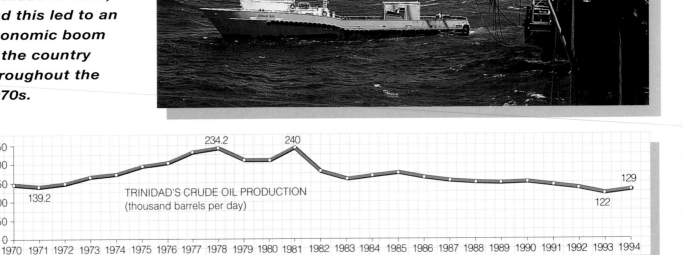

TRINIDAD'S CRUDE OIL PRODUCTION
(thousand barrels per day)

139.2 — 234.2 — 240 — 129 — 122

1970 1971 1972 1973 1974 1975 1976 1977 1978 1979 1980 1981 1982 1983 1984 1985 1986 1987 1988 1989 1990 1991 1992 1993 1994

islands with a degree of self-sufficiency include Barbados, which produces about 45% of its oil needs and all its natural gas, and Cuba, which meets about 10% of its oil demand.

HYDRO-ELECTRICITY, solar and wind energy are relatively undeveloped. This is because most of the islands' rivers are too small to support hydro-electric projects, although Cuba, Dominica, the Dominican Republic, Haiti and Jamaica all have small schemes. Solar and wind power require large amounts of space, which many islands do not have. Even where they do, it is expensive to collect and store such energy and not enough is produced for industrial purposes. Much of the region relies on wood and charcoal for domestic energy. This leads to forest loss and erosion, but many people cannot afford the alternatives, such as bottled gas and paraffin.

◀ *A hydro-electric dam at Pelgré in Haiti. Deforestation and subsequent erosion along the river feeding the dam has caused the reservoir to fill up with top-soil – a process known as siltation.*

POPULATION

In 1996, the Caribbean population was approximately 36 million, with 90% living on just five islands – Cuba, Dominican Republic, Haiti, Puerto Rico and Jamaica. Cuba, the most heavily populated island, has nearly 11 million people compared with Anguilla, which has only 10,000 inhabitants. Because the size of the population is closely related to the size of the island, population density is a better measure of how populated each island is. This ranges from 19 people per square kilometre in The Bahamas to 598 per square kilometre in Barbados.

The Caribbean population is growing at an average 1.5–2.0% per year. This means it will double in 34–46 years, if those rates

▲ **Squatter settlements like this one, in Haiti, are home to many of the poorest people in the Caribbean islands. They lack services like electricity, piped water, sewerage and refuse collection.**

POPULATION
annual growth rate,
1980-95 (%)

0.7	Anguilla
0.9	Cuba
2.1	Dominican Republic
2	Haiti
0.9	Jamaica
1.3	Trinidad & Tobago
1	USA
0.2	UK

▶ **Children in a slum in Havana, Cuba. A high proportion of the population in this region are under the age of 15.**

continue. Some islands such as Grenada, Haiti and St Lucia have over 40% of their population under the age of 15. When these young people have children of their own it will have a considerable effect on the rate of population growth. By contrast, only around 25% of the population in Cuba, Barbados and Martinique are under 15, but

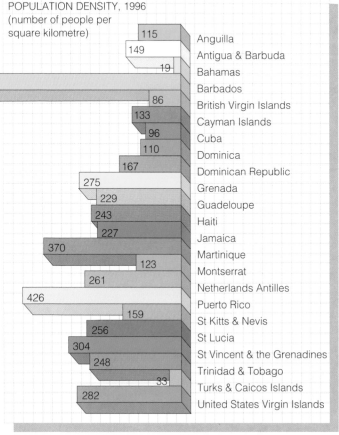

POPULATION DENSITY, 1996
(number of people per square kilometre)

Anguilla	115
Antigua & Barbuda	149
Bahamas	19
Barbados	598
British Virgin Islands	86
Cayman Islands	133
Cuba	96
Dominica	110
Dominican Republic	167
Grenada	275
Guadeloupe	229
Haiti	243
Jamaica	227
Martinique	370
Montserrat	123
Netherlands Antilles	261
Puerto Rico	426
St Kitts & Nevis	159
St Lucia	256
St Vincent & the Grenadines	304
Trinidad & Tobago	248
Turks & Caicos Islands	33
United States Virgin Islands	282

this is still a higher proportion than in Europe and North America where the figure is around 20%.

ETHNIC GROUPS AND LANGUAGES

The Caribbean's long and changing history is largely responsible for its truly COSMOPOLITAN population of today. The native Carib and Arawak people were largely wiped out with the arrival of the Europeans in the 16th century. The islands soon became populated with millions of West Africans who were shipped over as slaves for European sugar plantations. When slavery was eventually abolished in the 19th century, the African immigrants rebelled and the Europeans turned to India and China to supply INDENTURED LABOURERS for their estates. Immigration from India

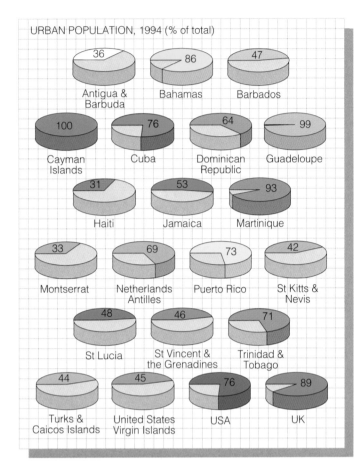

URBAN POPULATION, 1994 (% of total)

Island	%
Antigua & Barbuda	36
Bahamas	86
Barbados	47
Cayman Islands	100
Cuba	76
Dominican Republic	64
Guadeloupe	99
Haiti	31
Jamaica	53
Martinique	93
Montserrat	33
Netherlands Antilles	69
Puerto Rico	73
St Kitts & Nevis	42
St Lucia	48
St Vincent & the Grenadines	46
Trinidad & Tobago	71
Turks & Caicos Islands	44
United States Virgin Islands	45
USA	76
UK	89

was particularly high and they became known as East Indians to distinguish them from the West Indians already living in the Caribbean. All these periods of history are reflected in the cosmopolitan population of the region and nowhere more than in Trinidad and Tobago. These islands are among the most ethnically diverse countries in the world. Many of today's population are of mixed race, such as the Afro-Europeans or Afro-East Indians. In the Dominican Republic, mixed races account for 73% of the population. The major languages in the region are English, Spanish and Creole. French and Dutch are spoken on islands such as Martinique and the Netherlands Antilles. Creole is a language that was developed to make it possible for people from several language groups to communicate in a common language. In the Caribbean, its origins can be traced to English, French and Spanish.

◄ *A unique feature of the seafront in Willemstad, Curaçao, in the Netherlands Antilles are these 17th-century buildings built by the Dutch settlers.*

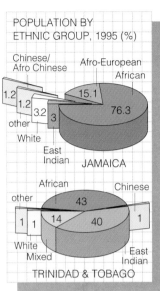

POPULATION BY
ETHNIC GROUP, 1995 (%)

Chinese/
Afro Chinese

Afro-European

African

1.2

1.2

3.2

3

15.1

76.3

other

White

East
Indian

JAMAICA

African

Chinese

other

1

1

14

43

40

1

White

Mixed

East
Indian

TRINIDAD & TOBAGO

KEY FACTS

● In 1996 the Caribbean population was estimated to be 35,734,288, which is about twice the population of New York state or 60% of the UK population.
● Average population density in the Caribbean is 150 per square kilometre compared with 68 per square kilometre in Europe and 28 per square kilometre in the USA.
● Haiti has only 1 doctor for every 7,000 people compared with the UK, which has 1 doctor for every 300 people.

MIGRATION

West Indian people are nearly all descended from migrants and, today, they are still a population on the move. In the early twentieth century, many left to find work and helped in the building of America's railways and the construction

▲ *A Carnival street parade at Castries in St Lucia. The Caribbean is home to people from many different ethnic backgrounds.*

of the Panama Canal which links the Atlantic and Pacific Oceans. In the 1950s, thousands of West Indians migrated to the UK to fill a demand for workers in hospitals, restaurants and public transport. Of the 12,000 people living in Montserrat at the time, 4,000 emigrated and by 1970, 300,000 Jamaicans (about 15% of the population) had moved to the UK. Although emigration eased pressures in the Caribbean and provided valuable income as people sent money home, it also led to a more harmful 'brain drain' of skilled people such as doctors and teachers which continues today. Immigration to the Caribbean is generally low, although The Bahamas and the US Virgin Islands attract people from neighbouring islands with their higher standard of living and low taxes.

◀ *This old board house in Jamaica is typical of rural housing in the Caribbean islands.*

▼ *Luxury residential areas such as this one in Kingston, Jamaica, are home to a small proportion of the population. Many of them have satellite televisions, swimming pools and employ domestic staff.*

Because life in the various islands can be so different, it is difficult to write about people's daily lives in general terms. Haiti, for example, is the poorest nation in the Western Hemisphere, with a 1995 per capita income of just US$ 250, while the Cayman Islands enjoy a per capita income of about US$ 22,500. This is more than in the UK or Canada. On Guadeloupe, 99% of the population live in towns and cities, but the urban population is only 36% in Antigua and Barbuda.

URBAN LIFE

Over the whole region, 60% of the population live in towns and cities, working in offices and banks, shops and restaurants, on public transport and in the hotel and tourism industry. The banking sector is particularly important and many people earn high incomes, and can afford to live in luxury houses with cars and domestic servants. The majority earn low incomes and live in cramped and often low-quality housing.

RURAL LIFE

The majority of the Caribbean's poor live in rural areas. It is no coincidence that Haiti, with the highest proportion of rural population at around 70%, is also the

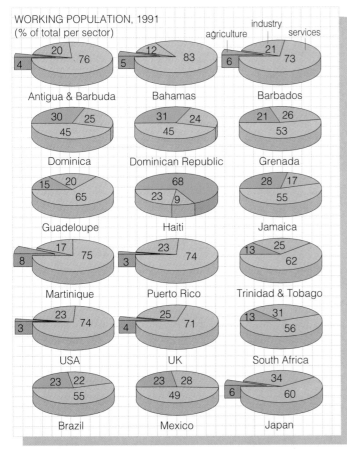

WORKING POPULATION, 1991
(% of total per sector)

agriculture   industry   services

20 / 76 / 4	12 / 83 / 5	21 / 73 / 6
Antigua & Barbuda	Bahamas	Barbados
30 / 25 / 45	31 / 24 / 45	21 / 26 / 53
Dominica	Dominican Republic	Grenada
15 / 20 / 65	68 / 23 / 9	28 / 17 / 55
Guadeloupe	Haiti	Jamaica
17 / 75 / 8	23 / 74 / 3	13 / 25 / 62
Martinique	Puerto Rico	Trinidad & Tobago
23 / 74 / 3	25 / 71 / 4	13 / 31 / 56
USA	UK	South Africa
23 / 22 / 55	23 / 28 / 49	34 / 60 / 6
Brazil	Mexico	Japan

poorest, with an estimated 76% of the population living in poverty. Most rural dwellers farm their own land, or work on plantations producing export crops such as sugar cane and bananas. Children are an important part of the rural economy, helping around the house, in the fields, or by taking produce to markets.

EDUCATION

Throughout the Caribbean, education is free and compulsory for children up to around 11 or 12 years old. On some islands, such as Barbados, it is compulsory up to the age of 16. The proportion of children who complete primary schooling varies dramatically, from over 95% in Jamaica and Trinidad and Tobago, to just 47% in Haiti – one of the lowest rates in the world. Enrolment in secondary schools also varies, at only 22% in Haiti, compared with around 75% in Trinidad and Tobago. With

◄ *Dominoes is a popular pastime in the Caribbean islands. These players are in Santo Domingo, in the Dominican Republic.*

DAILY LIFE

▶ *Education is free and compulsory on all of the islands. These girls at Mandeville, Jamaica, work and play during their lunchtime break.*

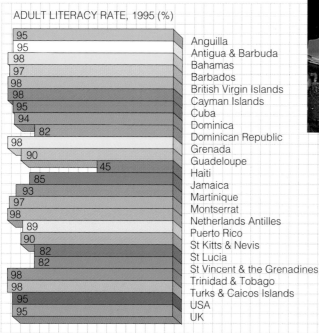

ADULT LITERACY RATE, 1995 (%)

95	Anguilla
95	Antigua & Barbuda
98	Bahamas
97	Barbados
98	British Virgin Islands
98	Cayman Islands
95	Cuba
94	Dominica
82	Dominican Republic
98	Grenada
90	Guadeloupe
45	Haiti
85	Jamaica
93	Martinique
97	Montserrat
98	Netherlands Antilles
89	Puerto Rico
90	St Kitts & Nevis
82	St Lucia
82	St Vincent & the Grenadines
98	Trinidad & Tobago
98	Turks & Caicos Islands
95	USA
95	UK

▼ *A church service in Bridgetown, Barbados. The Church plays an important part in many peoples' lives, especially in rural areas.*

the exception of Haiti, the large numbers of children attending school are responsible for the Caribbean's high adult literacy rates, which are above those of many other developing parts of the world.

RELIGION

Christianity is the main religion of the Caribbean, although it is split into many denominations. Hinduism and Islam are significant on islands with East Indian

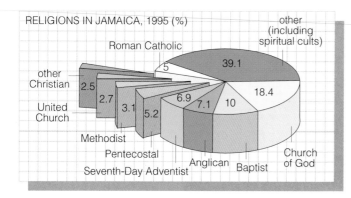

RELIGIONS IN JAMAICA, 1995 (%)

Roman Catholic — 5
other (including spiritual cults) — 39.1
other Christian — 2.5
United Church — 2.7
Methodist — 3.1
Pentecostal — 5.2
Seventh-Day Adventist — 6.9
Anglican — 7.1
Baptist — 10
Church of God — 18.4

communities, like Trinidad where 25% of the population are Hindus and 6% Moslems. There are also spiritual religions related to African beliefs, like voodoo in Haiti. In Jamaica, the Rastafarian religion has a strong following.

▲ *The West Indies have produced many world-class cricketers like Sir Gary Sobers, Viv Richards and Brian Lara. This match in St Kitts was played during an Australian tour to the Caribbean.*

KEY FACTS

● The reggae group, Bob Marley and the Wailers, were so influential that they even played in Zimbabwe's independence ceremony in 1980. Sadly, Bob Marley died the following year of cancer, aged just 36.

● The oldest university in the Western Hemisphere, the Autonomous University of Santo Domingo, was founded in the Dominican Republic in 1538.

● The 1992 Nobel Prize for Literature was won by Derek Walcott, a St Lucian poet.

● Brian Lara, a cricket player from Trinidad, holds the world record for the highest ever innings (501 not out) and the highest test innings (375) for the West Indies against England.

CULTURAL LIFE AND SPORT

Music and dance are central to Caribbean culture and the strong Caribbean rhythms have influenced musicians all over the world. Reggae music is the most famous. Trinidad is the home of calypso music and, in the 1930s, its musicians turned old oil barrels into musical drums to give birth to the music of steel bands. The influence of West African culture is strong, particularly so in Trinidad's world famous carnival.

Cricket is the most widely played sport and the West Indies team is among the finest in the world. The islands have also produced the world's greatest sprinters with the last three Olympic (100 metres) champions being Jamaican born, including Donovan Bailey (running for Canada) who broke the world record in the 1996 Games.

COLONIALISM

The modern Caribbean is characterized by a true mixture of ruling powers and political systems, but there is one element all the islands have shared – colonialism. In the 17th and 18th centuries Britain, France, Spain the Netherlands, and Denmark all struggled for a share of the Caribbean. Some islands changed hands several times. Tobago, for example, was occupied by the British, Dutch, and French during the 17th century. The USA also intervened, taking control of Puerto Rico after the Spanish–American War of 1898. In 1917, the USA bought the Virgin Islands from the Danish for US$ 25 million, as a strategic point for shipping traffic between the Atlantic Ocean and the Panama Canal.

▲ *Government House, Nassau, in The Bahamas. The Bahamas is one of eight parliamentary monarchies in the Caribbean whose governments are modelled on the British constitutional pattern.*

INDEPENDENCE

Haiti was the first of the islands to gain independence in 1804, following a successful revolt by former slaves against the French. The Spanish colonies of the Dominican Republic and Cuba followed in 1865 and 1898 respectively. There were no further changes until after the Second World War. Then, in 1946, the French islands (Guadeloupe and Martinique) were incorporated into the metropolitan power and, in 1954, the Dutch made the

Netherlands Antilles a dependency. The British gave independence to Jamaica and Trinidad and Tobago in 1962, and, later, to most of their other colonies. Eight of them became parliamentary monarchies, with the British monarch as their head of state, while two (Dominica and Trinidad and Tobago) became parliamentary republics with an elected President. All of them became members of the Commonwealth. Five of the former British colonies, including the Cayman Islands and

Montserrat, are now dependent territories. This means they are represented by a Governor, who manages most of their internal affairs. Britain however, is still responsible for foreign policy and defence and the British monarch remains the head of state.

THE REPUBLICS

There are three Caribbean republics with elected Presidents as their head of state. Cuba is a one-party Communist state which means that, although there are elections, the candidates are all representatives of the Communist party. The Dominican Republic and Haiti are both democracies with several parties, but they have been plagued by oppressive dictators and COUPS D'ÉTAT. The USA has intervened in the politics of both islands

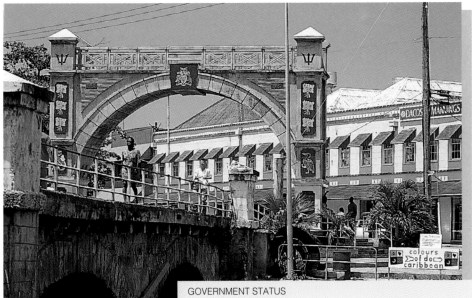

▲ Independence Arch, Bridgetown, Barbados. The island achieved independence from Britain in 1966.

GOVERNMENT STATUS			
Country	Status	Since	Former status
ANGUILLA	British Dependent Territory	1982	British colony
ANTIGUA & BARBUDA	Parliamentary monarchy	1981	British colony
BAHAMAS	Parliamentary monarchy	1973	British colony
BARBADOS	Parliamentary monarchy	1966	British colony
BRITISH VIRGIN ISLANDS	British Dependent Territory	1960	British colony
CAYMAN ISLANDS	British Dependent Territory	1962	British colony
CUBA	Republic	1898	Spanish colony
DOMINICA	Parliamentary republic	1978	British colony
DOMINICAN REPUBLIC	Republic	1865	Spanish colony
GRENADA	Parliamentary monarchy	1974	British colony
GUADELOUPE	Overseas Department of France	1946	French colony
HAITI	Republic	1804	French colony
JAMAICA	Parliamentary monarchy	1962	British colony
MARTINIQUE	Overseas Department of France	1946	French colony
MONTSERRAT	British Dependent Territory	1960	British colony
NETHERLANDS ANTILLES	Netherlands Dependencies	1954	Dutch colony
PUERTO RICO	Self-governing commonwealth	1952	US possession
ST KITTS & NEVIS	Parliamentary monarchy	1983	British colony
ST LUCIA	Parliamentary monarchy	1979	British colony
ST VINCENT & THE GRENADINES	Parliamentary monarchy	1979	British colony
TRINIDAD & TOBAGO	Parliamentary republic	1962	British colony
TURKS & CAICOS ISLANDS	British Dependent Territory	1972	British colony
UNITED STATES VIRGIN ISLANDS	US External Territory	1917	Danish colony

▼ *A policeman emerges from the Gendarmerie Nationale in Terre-de-Haut, Guadeloupe. Guadeloupe is governed as a district of France.*

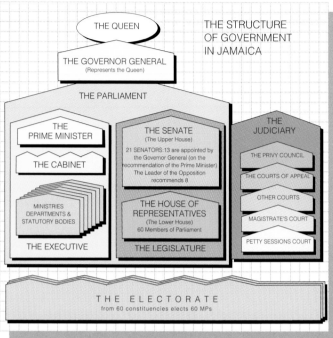

THE QUEEN

THE GOVERNOR GENERAL
(Represents the Queen)

THE STRUCTURE
OF GOVERNMENT
IN JAMAICA

THE PARLIAMENT

THE PRIME MINISTER

THE CABINET

MINISTRIES
DEPARTMENTS &
STATUTORY BODIES

THE EXECUTIVE

THE SENATE
(The Upper House)
21 SENATORS:13 are appointed by
the Governor General (on the
recommendation of the Prime Minister)
The Leader of the Opposition
recommends 8

THE HOUSE OF
REPRESENTATIVES
(The Lower House)
60 Members of Parliament

THE LEGISLATURE

THE JUDICIARY

THE PRIVY COUNCIL

THE COURTS OF APPEAL

OTHER COURTS

MAGISTRATE'S COURT

PETTY SESSIONS COURT

THE ELECTORATE
from 60 constituencies elects 60 MPs

on several occasions, most recently sending troops into the Dominican Republic in 1965, and Haiti in 1994, to restore stability and democracy.

OVERSEAS CONNECTIONS

Largely due to their colonial history, the modern states of the Caribbean maintain close overseas connections. The Netherlands Antilles maintain a Dutch legal system, the people of Guadeloupe and Martinique have the same rights and obligations as French citizens, and the

KEY FACTS

● In 1804, Haiti became the first Caribbean country to achieve independence, and the first black republic in the world.

● In 1983 and 1994, US troops invaded Grenada and Haiti following coups d'état.

● In 1958 most British West Indian islands formed the Federation of the West Indies. It did not survive: in 1962 Jamaica and Trinidad and Tobago became independent.

● The age of voting is 18 in all of the Caribbean islands except Cuba where people can vote at 16.

● In the early 1980s, the US Embassy estimated that Jamaica earned US$ 1.5 billion from the illegal export of marijuana (cannabis). This led to a major clamp down on illegal producers in the island.

● Puerto Ricans share most of the rights of other US citizens but pay no federal taxes and cannot vote in elections for the US President or Congress.

▶ *Troops patrolling the streets in Haiti. In the 20th century, the island has been ruled by dictators and has suffered from political unrest.*

▼ *An election rally in support of the National Front for Change and Democracy (FNCD), in Port-au-Prince, Haiti.*

former British colonies operate legal systems based on English Law. Puerto Rico is a self-governing commonwealth, in a free political association with the USA, and its citizens are US citizens. The people of the US Virgin Islands are also US citizens and operate a legal system based on US law. In Cuba, the Marxist leader Fidel Castro developed strong links with the former USSR and other Marxist leaders in Africa and the Middle East, causing many western nations to impose trade sanctions and halt diplomatic relations with Cuba.

ILLICIT DRUGS

One of the major law and order issues today is the involvement of some of the islands, such as Dominica, Haiti, Jamaica and the Netherlands Antilles, in the illegal trafficking of drugs between South America and the USA and Europe. Jamaica illegally produces cannabis. The government, with the help of the US Drug Enforcement Agency (DEA), is currently trying to combat this problem.

FOOD AND FARMING

CASH CROPS

During colonial rule, the development of large scale commercial farming in the Caribbean shaped many of the islands' economies. Today, crops such as sugar cane, bananas, coffee, cocoa, citrus fruits and tobacco are grown on large estates as 'cash crops' for the world markets. Sugar cane is the most important crop and is grown on all the large islands and also on Barbados and St Kitts. In Jamaica, 20% of the land area is devoted to growing sugar cane. The industry employs 60,000 people (7% of the workforce) and generates around 4% of export earnings. Bananas are the Caribbean's second major export crop and are particularly important for Dominica,

BANANA PRODUCTION, 1996 (thousand tonnes)

116	130	135			160
Guadeloupe	Jamaica	St Lucia			Cuba

210	239	361	5,309	5,692	9,935
Martinique	Haiti	Dominican Republic	Ecuador	Brazil	India

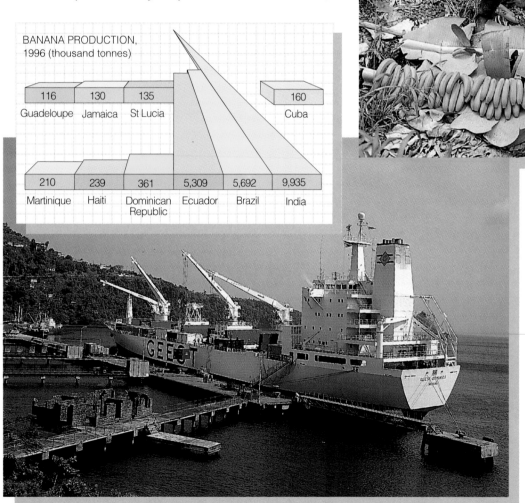

▲ *Cutting bananas for export in St Lucia. The banana is a large tree-like herbacious plant, whose thin stem is wrapped in a sheaf of overlapping leaves.*

◀ *The arrival of the large white Geest Industries freighter in Kingstown Harbour is an important weekly event in St Vincent.*

KEY FACTS

● The weather can seriously disrupt Caribbean agriculture. In 1995, 20% of St Lucia's banana crop was destroyed by tropical storm Iris, and hurricanes Luis and Marilyn destroyed virtually all of Dominica's banana crop.

● The US Virgin Islands does not have enough farmland to be self-sufficient in food and imports most of its food from the USA. The Cayman Islands imports around 90% of its food.

● The Dominican Republic produced 46,652 tonnes of coffee in 1996 and is the region's biggest producer. Jamaica produced only 2,580 tonnes but its Blue Mountain coffee is said to be among the best (and most expensive) in the world.

● In 1991, nearly 35% of Haiti's GROSS DOMESTIC PRODUCT (GDP) was from the agricultural sector and it employed 66% of the island's labour force.

St Lucia and St Vincent. The Dominican Republic and Haiti are the region's leading producers and, in 1996, produced 361,047 and 239,200 tonnes respectively. St Lucia produced around 135,000 tonnes which accounted for over 50% of its export earnings. It can be risky for an island to rely heavily on a single crop, because world demand can vary, and weather, disease or pests can destroy the crop. Increased production of bananas in South America has already lowered the market price and, in 1995, many of the islands had their crop partially destroyed in a series of tropical storms.

Spices are an important part of Caribbean agriculture. Jamaica is a major producer of pimento (allspice), and Grenada is one of the world's largest nutmeg producers. Other spices grown in the region include cinnamon, cloves, ginger and various peppers. In recent years, Caribbean agriculture has expanded into horticulture – the production of fresh fruit, vegetables, plants and flowers. Jamaica and The

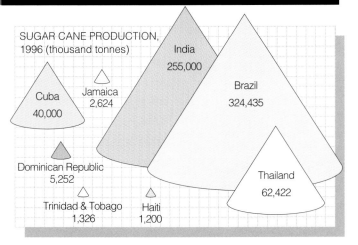

SUGAR CANE PRODUCTION, 1996 (thousand tonnes)

India 255,000

Brazil 324,435

Cuba 40,000

Jamaica 2,624

Dominican Republic 5,252

Thailand 62,422

Trinidad & Tobago 1,326

Haiti 1,200

▶ *Sugar-cane at a factory in Jamaica. The cane is washed, shredded, then crushed to extract the juice. The juice is boiled, and the water evaporates, leaving crystals of brown sugar.*

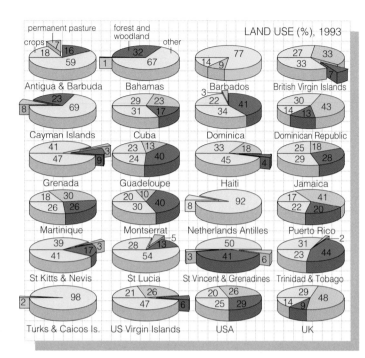

LAND USE (%), 1993

permanent pasture	crops	forest and woodland	other

Antigua & Barbuda: crops 7, permanent pasture 18, 16, 59

Bahamas: 1, forest and woodland 32, 67

Barbados: 77, 14, 9

British Virgin Islands: 27, 33, 33, 7

Cayman Islands: 23, 8, 69

Cuba: 29, 23, 31, 17

Dominica: 3, 22, 34, 41

Dominican Republic: 30, 14, 13, 43

Grenada: 41, 47, 3, 9

Guadeloupe: 23, 13, 24, 40

Haiti: 33, 18, 45, 4

Jamaica: 25, 18, 29, 28

Martinique: 18, 30, 26, 26

Montserrat: 20, 10, 30, 40

Netherlands Antilles: 8, 92

Puerto Rico: 17, 41, 22, 20

St Kitts & Nevis: 39, 17, 3, 41

St Lucia: 28, 13, 5, 54

St Vincent & Grenadines: 50, 3, 41, 6

Trinidad & Tobago: 31, 2, 23, 44

Turks & Caicos Is.: 2, 98

US Virgin Islands: 21, 26, 47, 6

USA: 20, 26, 25, 29

UK: 29, 48, 14, 9

Bahamas supply cucumbers and tomatoes to the USA market, while Puerto Rico and Jamaica have successfully entered the international market for houseplants and flowers.

LOCAL FOOD AND FARMING

The staple foods of the Caribbean include yams, cassava, potatoes, sweet potatoes, plantains, breadfruit and various vegetables. These are normally grown on smallholdings of up to 3 hectares and sold in lively and colourful markets. On the smaller plots, farmers may not produce a surplus for sale and the family will consume all of what is grown. This is called

◄ *Yams, carrots, cucumbers, tomatoes, pumpkins and peppers are some of the vegetables offered for sale at markets throughout the Caribbean. Food crops are mostly produced by small farmers, who sell their surplus at markets like this one.*

◄ *A seine net is drawn in on the beach in Grenada. When a catch is landed, family members help the fishermen to sort and sell the fish. Fishing in the Caribbean is insignificant in world terms, but fish are an important part of the local diet.*

SUBSISTENCE FARMING and, in Haiti, it accounts for the majority of the 66% of the workforce working on the land. Many farmers will grow several crops on their land at the same time, a technique known as INTERCROPPING. This ensures a continuous supply of food throughout the year. It also helps to protect against drought or disease, as some plants will be more resistant than others. Livestock farming is not important in the region, although cattle are kept on Puerto Rico, Jamaica, and Trinidad. Smaller livestock such as goats, pigs and chickens are often kept to meet people's own requirements.

Despite being surrounded by sea, most of the region's fish is imported, with only The Bahamas being self-sufficient. The Caribbean Sea lacks nutrients, and the best fishing grounds, such as those around Jamaica, have been over-exploited and almost fished out.

In Caribbean cooking, roots, vegetables, fruits, spices, fish, chicken and goat are used in a variety of dishes influenced by Indian, African, European and American tastes. A local snack food, roti, is particularly common. It is a spicy curried filling (often potato and chicken) rolled in a tortilla-like bread and can be bought very cheaply.

Limited farmland means that much of the Caribbean's food is imported. Islands such as the Cayman Islands and the Turks and Caicos Islands rely almost entirely on imported foodstuffs from the USA, UK and neighbouring islands. Beef and dairy products are particularly scarce and account for around 35% of the import bill. A severe strain can be placed on the economy of a country that is forced to rely on imports for basic needs, often leading to large debts.

The Caribbean is dominated by a single industry – tourism. The tropical climate, friendly people, and beautiful scenery attract millions of tourists every year from all over the world. Puerto Rico and The Bahamas are the main tourist destinations and, in 1994, they attracted over 3 million, and 1.5 million visitors respectively. Tourism is even more important in the smaller islands, such as the Cayman and US Virgin Islands, where it accounts for about 70% of GDP. Tourism is still growing rapidly in many islands. This stimulates growth in other sectors that support tourism, such as the

▲ *Cruise ships dock at Charlotte Amalie, St Thomas, in the US Virgin Islands. Each ship brings hundreds of tourists.*

▶ *Dunn's River Falls is Jamaica's main tourist attraction. About a million people visit it every year.*

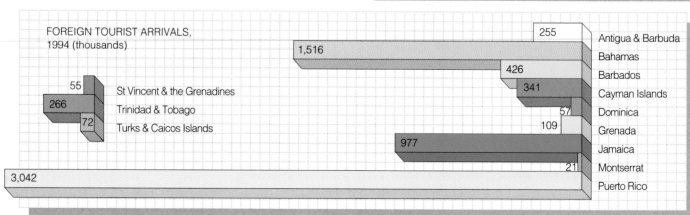

FOREIGN TOURIST ARRIVALS, 1994 (thousands)

Island	Arrivals
Antigua & Barbuda	255
Bahamas	1,516
Barbados	426
Cayman Islands	341
Dominica	57
Grenada	109
Jamaica	977
Montserrat	21
Puerto Rico	3,042
St Vincent & the Grenadines	55
Trinidad & Tobago	266
Turks & Caicos Islands	72

construction, catering and transport industries. As agricultural prices fall, tourist earnings are becoming increasingly important for islands like Martinique and St Kitts and Nevis.

MANUFACTURING

Manufacturing is expanding in the region but is, so far, limited to a few key industries. Rum is distilled from molasses (a by-product of the sugar industry) on many islands. Cement is produced in Barbados, Cuba, and Trinidad. Jamaica produces alumina, from bauxite, for use in the production of aluminium. One of the biggest industries in the region is the petro-chemical industry. Trinidad uses its petroleum resources in the manufacture of detergents, fertilizers, paints, plastics,

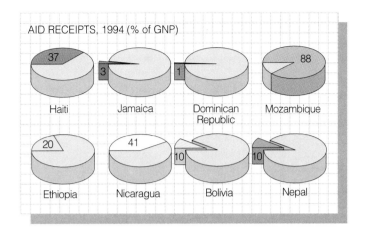

AID RECEIPTS, 1994 (% of GNP)

Haiti 37 — Jamaica 3 — Dominican Republic 1 — Mozambique 88 — Ethiopia 20 — Nicaragua 41 — Bolivia 10 — Nepal 10

solvents and pharmaceuticals. Other islands, like Jamaica and the US Virgin Islands, have petroleum refineries for the processing of imported oil.

FREE TRADE ZONES have helped to encourage the growth of manufacturing on several islands. Overseas firms are attracted by low wages, the lack of trade

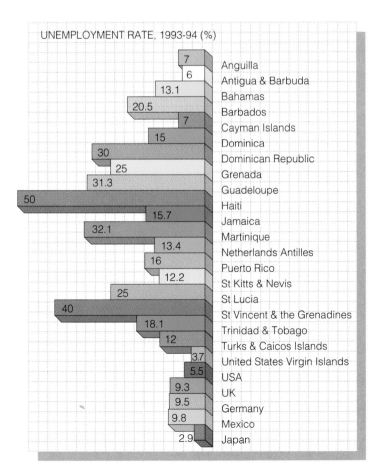

UNEMPLOYMENT RATE, 1993-94 (%)

Anguilla	7
Antigua & Barbuda	6
Bahamas	13.1
Barbados	20.5
Cayman Islands	7
Dominica	15
Dominican Republic	30
Grenada	25
Guadeloupe	31.3
Haiti	50
Jamaica	15.7
Martinique	32.1
Netherlands Antilles	13.4
Puerto Rico	16
St Kitts & Nevis	12.2
St Lucia	25
St Vincent & the Grenadines	40
Trinidad & Tobago	18.1
Turks & Caicos Islands	12
United States Virgin Islands	3.7
USA	5.5
UK	9.3
Germany	9.5
Mexico	9.8
Japan	2.9

▲ *A Rastafarian craftsman making leather boots in St Kitts.*

▲ *Cloth is painted with wax, as part of the process of making batik, at a small factory in Grenada.*

unions and low taxation levels. Electronics, textiles and consumer goods are produced, and usually sold in American or European markets. Puerto Rico has the most diverse manufacturing economy, producing more than all the other islands combined. It benefits from close trading relations with the USA which mean its products are exempt from US import taxes. Companies from the USA have also invested heavily in Puerto Rico since the 1950s, to make manufacturing its most important sector, accounting for 42% of GDP.

Offshore financial services are a growing part of Caribbean economies, particularly in Anguilla, The Bahamas, the Cayman Islands, the Netherlands Antilles and the Turks and Caicos. These islands are attractive because of their low taxation levels and stable political and economic climate. The Cayman Islands is a particularly important centre for financial services and, as a result, its residents today enjoy one of the highest standards of living in the world.

IMPORTS AND EXPORTS, 1995 (US$ millions)

imports				exports
653	Barbados	168		
1,868	Guadeloupe	162		
2,773	Jamaica		1,429	
1,969	Martinique	242		
1,723	Trinidad & Tobago		2,467	

KEY FACTS

● Tourism in the Turks and Caicos islands grew by about 10% in 1995, with most visitors (60,000 or 70%) coming from the USA.
● Cruise ships are important to Caribbean tourism. In 1994, cruise arrivals in Antigua increased by 17% on the previous year.
● The petroleum refinery at Saint Croix in the US Virgin Islands is one of the largest in the world.
● Jamaica's clothing industry employed 9,000 people in 1984, but by 1994 had expanded to 44,000. It accounted for US$ 450 million in export earnings.
● The fall in banana prices in 1993, led to riots in St Lucia, St Vincent and the Grenadines. The changes in the industry are likely to lead to 4,000–8,000 job losses on each of the islands.

◀ *The Hato Rey
financial area in
San Juan, Puerto
Rico. Puerto Rico
has one of the
most dynamic
economies in the
Caribbean region.*

▶*In Puerto Rico, industry
is a more important
economic activity than
agriculture. This distillery
in San Juan produces rum.*

TRADE AGREEMENTS

The Caribbean islands benefit from
several trade agreements similar to those
of the European Union (EU) or the North
American Free Trade Agreement (NAFTA).
The Caribbean Basin Initiative (CBI) allows
various Caribbean goods to enter the US
market duty free. The Caribbean Common
Market (CARICOM) allows free trade
between its member countries. The
Organization of the Eastern Caribbean
States (OECS), which is made up of
Antigua and Barbuda, Dominica, Grenada,
St Kitts and Nevis, St Lucia and St Vincent
and the Grenadines, was formed in 1981
as a group within the larger CARICOM.
These islands have small populations,
a limited land area and rely heavily on
imported goods. They share a common
currency (the East Caribbean Dollar),
a central bank, and a central planning
authority which means they can compete
more effectively in the international markets.
One of the recent problems facing the
OECS has been the decline in world banana
prices since 1992 and the possible loss of
the European market for its bananas, after
2001, to South American producers.

TRANSPORT

ransport links are vital to small island economies like the Caribbean. Shipping is important for the export of minerals and agricultural goods, and the import of foodstuffs, consumer goods and fuel. As the cruise industry expands, the seas also bring hundreds of thousands of tourists every year. The Caribbean is also the main route for international shipping travelling through the Panama Canal, linking the Atlantic and Pacific Oceans. Virtually all the islands have ports. The largest ones capable of handling container ships are TRANS-SHIPMENT PORTS, such as San Juan in Puerto Rico and Port of Spain in Trinidad.

Air travel is replacing much of the shipping traffic, particularly for the export of fresh fruit and vegetables, and for people travelling both between islands and internationally. Local airports service regional flights operated by several airlines while the larger

KEY FACTS

● In Haiti only 944 kilometres of the 3,978 kilometre road network is paved. Barbados has the only entirely paved network with 1,550 kilometres of roads.
● All the islands have at least one airport. Cuba has 181 and The Bahamas has 60.
● Jamaica's Kingston Harbour is the seventh largest natural harbour in the world.
● The Caribbean Sea is a major trade route for Latin American countries. The Windward Passage, between Cuba and Haiti, is a major shipping route between the USA and the Panama Canal.

islands such as the Dominican Republic and Haiti have international airports, with connections to the USA, Europe and beyond.

Local travel is mainly by road, using buses, trucks and taxis. The road network

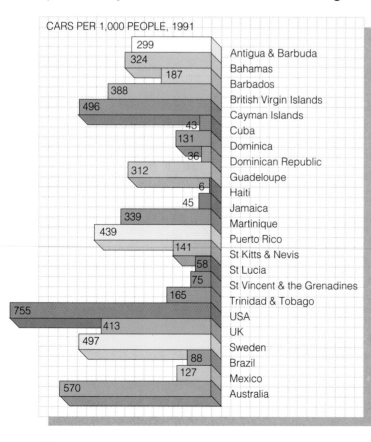

CARS PER 1,000 PEOPLE, 1991

299	Antigua & Barbuda
324	Bahamas
187	Barbados
388	British Virgin Islands
496	Cayman Islands
43	Cuba
131	Dominica
36	Dominican Republic
312	Guadeloupe
6	Haiti
45	Jamaica
339	Martinique
439	Puerto Rico
141	St Kitts & Nevis
58	St Lucia
75	St Vincent & the Grenadines
165	Trinidad & Tobago
755	USA
413	UK
497	Sweden
88	Brazil
127	Mexico
570	Australia

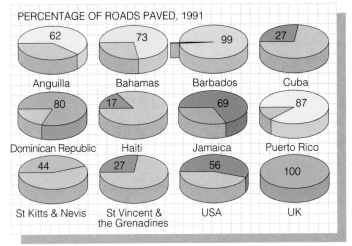

◀ *Air Jamaica operates over 100 flights a week to the USA, Canada and the UK. Jamaica has two international airports – in Kingston and Montego Bay.*

originally linked the plantations to the ports, but has now expanded to link most towns. The use of private vehicles is limited due to their expense, although wealthier countries, such as the Cayman islands and Puerto Rico, have a higher proportion of private car use than the UK. Smaller mountainous states, like Dominica, St Vincent and the Grenadines, are hampered in their road network by the nature of their landscape, which makes roads expensive to build and maintain.

A few railways exist to transport goods such as sugar cane and bauxite to factories and the ports but, in many cases, these are being replaced by road transport. Only Cuba has a full passenger rail network. For many in rural areas, the main means of transport continues to be by foot or perhaps on donkey, using local footpaths and tracks.

PERCENTAGE OF ROADS PAVED, 1991

Anguilla	Bahamas	Barbados	Cuba
62	73	99	27

Dominican Republic	Haiti	Jamaica	Puerto Rico
80	17	69	87

St Kitts & Nevis	St Vincent & the Grenadines	USA	UK
44	27	56	100

◀ *Girls riding home from the farm on heavily laden donkeys in Haiti.*

▶ *Trucks and buses, like this one on St Kitts, are the most important form of transport on the islands. They are often dangerously crowded.*

THE ENVIRONMENT

The impact of humans on the environment can be particularly obvious on small islands like those of the Caribbean. Where land is limited, population pressure is a major cause of environmental damage. The steep slopes of the Yallahs River Basin in Jamaica have been cleared of trees for growing export crops and vegetables for local consumption, as the population has expanded. This has meant that the erosion, which is already serious, has worsened and increased the risk of landslides and flooding.

The cutting down of trees for firewood and charcoal production has had a major impact on upland areas of the Caribbean, particularly those in Haiti and the Dominican Republic. Antigua and Barbuda, Cuba, St Lucia and Trinidad also suffer from high rates of deforestation, as trees are cleared for agriculture, fuel and tourism development.

Industrial waste is an increasing problem as industry expands throughout the region. Mining, quarrying and oil refining have left their mark on parts of Cuba, the Dominican Republic, Jamaica and Trinidad. The waters of the region's main harbours are heavily polluted with industrial effluents. This pollution has spread to cause serious damage to coral reefs and beaches in the area, disrupting tourism and killing local fish. Ocean-going tourist liners have also been accused of damaging local marine life.

Fishing in the Caribbean has been so intensive that, in many areas, there are actually very few fish left. Fine-meshed nets

▼ *Factories close to the beach in Barbados risk polluting an important tourist resource.*

KEY FACTS

● Dominica's energy is produced mainly by hydro-electricity. Investment for this and for the island's water supply system is partly financed by the export of water to drier Caribbean islands, including Antigua.

● El Yunque is an 11,000-hectare rainforest, with more than 240 species of trees, in the Luquillo Mountains in Puerto Rico. It is the only tropical rainforest in the US National Forest system.

● The sea around The Bahamas is home to 5% of the world's coral. Coral absorbs carbon dioxide, just as the rainforests do.

● Jamaica has nearly 3,000 varieties of flowering plants, including 800 species found nowhere else in the world. 200 species of wild orchids are indigenous to the island.

● Every day, about 20 treatment plants dump 55,000,000 litres of sewage into Kingston Harbour, Jamaica.

● In 1993, Haiti used 6,171 cubic metres of local wood for fuel.

and fish pots mean that fish are caught very young, and often before they have bred, so that overall stocks are reduced. The technique of blasting fish out of the coral with explosives has also seriously damaged not just fish populations, but also the environment for lobsters, conch, sea turtles and other marine species. In Jamaican waters, the pressures on fishing have been so high that the average fish catch per canoe declined from 2,500 kilograms in 1981, to just 1,000 kilograms in 1991.

Fresh water is in very short supply on smaller islands like the British Virgin Islands, the Cayman Islands and the Turks and Caicos Islands. Many rely on the collection of rainwater for the majority of their supplies. Even larger islands have limited water supplies. Periodic droughts, such as those in Puerto Rico, have sometimes led to water rationing.

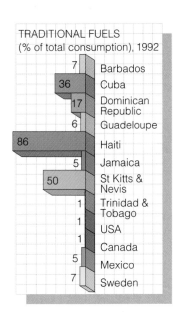

TRADITIONAL FUELS
(% of total consumption), 1992

	%	Country
	7	Barbados
	36	Cuba
	17	Dominican Republic
	6	Guadeloupe
	86	Haiti
	5	Jamaica
	50	St Kitts & Nevis
	1	Trinidad & Tobago
	1	USA
	1	Canada
	5	Mexico
	7	Sweden

▲ *A charcoal kiln in Jamaica. Some practices, such as felling wood for the manufacture of charcoal, contribute to deforestation and erosion in many islands.*

▼ *Lush tropical forest and bananas thrive on hillsides like this one in Puerto Rico. Many Caribbean governments have set up national parks to help protect the environment.*

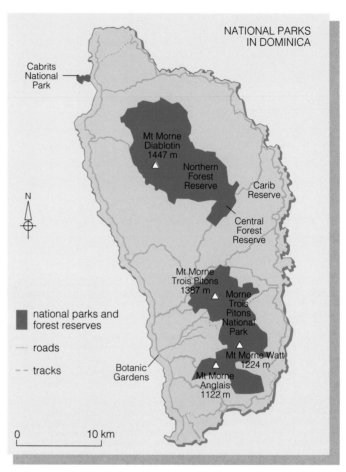

NATIONAL PARKS IN DOMINICA

Cabrits National Park

Mt Morne Diablotin 1447 m

Northern Forest Reserve

Carib Reserve

Central Forest Reserve

Mt Morne Trois Pitons 1387 m

Morne Trois Pitons National Park

Mt Morne Watt 1224 m

Mt Morne Anglais 1122 m

Botanic Gardens

N

■ national parks and forest reserves

---- roads

-- tracks

0   10 km

CONSERVATION

Despite its problems, the Caribbean is relatively unspoilt. Large parts still have the wooded mountains, white sandy beaches and clear seas that give the region its reputation as a tropical paradise. Governments recognize the value of the environment to tourism, and of tourism to the economy. They have, therefore, adopted policies to conserve their natural beauty and wildlife for future generations.

National parks are the main means of controlling human activity in fragile habitats. They also protect endangered plant and animal species. Guadeloupe has a 30,000-hectare rainforest reserve at the foot of La Soufrière. Two-thirds of the deep valleys and most of the shoreline on the US Virgin island, St John, have been set aside as a national park. Dominica has protected large areas which provide a home to its prolific bird life, including several rare and endangered species. It also has marine parks, as do the Turks and Caicos Islands, where the government has set up underwater parks that protect over 800 kilometres of coral reef. The Jamaican

▲ *The queen angelfish is one of the many colourful species that inhabit the Caribbean reefs.*

◀ *Tobago's blue-crowned motmot is one of Trinidad and Tobago's three national birds.*

government established a National Resource Conservation Project in 1991, and works with a non-government organization (NGO), the Jamaican Conservation and Development Trust, to protect its habitats and species. Jamaica has also been a leader in the United Nations (UN) International Seabed Authority (ISA) which aims to manage marine resources more efficiently. Following the Law of the Sea Convention, which was passed in 1994, the ISA is to be based in Jamaica.

THE FUTURE

The Caribbean islands have made great progress in the last 50 years, mainly due to favourable trade terms for agricultural exports to the USA and Europe. In the 1960s and 1970s, many of the islands' GDPs grew by between 5% and 6% a year. However, in the 1980s, world prices for agricultural and industrial commodities fell. This, together with long periods of worldwide recession, has reversed economic growth in many islands.

Tourism has been growing rapidly since the 1970s and it continues to bring valuable income to the Caribbean. There is, however, some concern about how it may effect the environment and whether it is desirable for some island economies to be so dependent on the tourist trade.

Manufacturing and financial services have, however, begun to expand on many islands. Whatever direction the Caribbean takes, governments will need to make sure that future development does not harm the natural environment, or the limited resources on which many of its island economies rely so heavily.

KEY FACTS

● In the Dominican Republic, life expectancy is likely to rise from 60 years in 1970 to 77 years by 2025.

● The new Barahona International Airport in the Dominican Republic is expected to lead to a rapid growth in tourism along the south-west coast.

● A US$ 28.2 million health and population project, funded by The World Bank and The Inter-American Development Bank, intends to extend health services to Haiti's poor. It aims to reduce cases of tuberculosis by half between 1997 and 2000 and also to help with a national AIDS programme.

● Direct Foreign investment into Trinidad and Tobago increased from US$ 63 million in 1988 to US$ 415 million in 1994. Changes to local taxes are expected to increase investment even more in the future.

● In 1997, The World Bank stated that the Caribbean must aim to diversify its economy, attract foreign investment and create jobs. Telecommunications, financial services, high-tech manufacturing and data processing are all possible growth industries.

● Arecibo Observatory in Puerto Rico is the site of the largest radio telescope in the world.

◀ *Students learning keyboard-skills. On several islands, data processing and information-based services are new industries with great potential for growth.*

FURTHER INFORMATION

- ANGUILLA TOURIST OFFICE
3 Epirus Road, London SW6
Provides a map and brochures on Anguilla.
- ANTIGUA & BARBUDA HIGH COMMISSION
15 Thayer Street, London W1
Provides a map and brochures on Antigua & Barbuda.
- BAHAMAS HIGH COMMISSION
10 Chesterfield Street, London W1
Provides fact sheets and brochure on The Bahamas.
- BARBADOS HIGH COMMISSION
1 Great Russell Street, London WC1
Provides a map, fact sheets and brochure on Barbados.
- BRITISH VIRGIN ISLANDS TOURIST BOARD
110 St Martins Lane, London WC2
Provides a map and brochures on the British Virgin Islands.
- CAYMAN ISLANDS GOVERNMENT OFFICE
6 Arlington Street, London SW1
Provides a booklet on the Cayman Islands.
- CUBAN TOURIST OFFICE
167 High Holborn, London WC1
Provides brochures on Cuba.
- DOMINICA HIGH COMMISSION
1 Collingham Gardens, London SW5
Provides a map and a booklet on Dominica.
- FRENCH TOURIST OFFICE
179 Piccadilly, London W1
Provides maps and leaflets on Guadeloupe and Martinique.
- GRENADA NATIONAL TOURIST OFFICE
1 Collingham Gardens, London SW5
Provides a map, fact sheets and brochures on Grenada.

- JAMAICA TOURIST BOARD
1 Prince Consort Road, London SW7
Provides a map and booklet on Jamaica.
- ST KITTS & NEVIS TOURISM OFFICE
10 Kensington Court, London W8
Provides a map and brochure on St Kitts & Nevis.
- ST LUCIA TOURIST BOARD
421a Finchley Road, London NW3
Provides a map and brochure on St Lucia.
- TRINIDAD & TOBAGO HIGH COMMISSION,
42 Belgrave Square, London SW1
Provides a map and brochure on Trinidad & Tobago.
- TURKS & CAICOS ISLANDS INFORMATION OFFICE
47 Chase Side, Enfield, Middx EN2 6NB
Provides a brochure with maps on Turks & Caicos Islands.
- UNITED STATES VIRGIN ISLES DIVISION OF TOURISM
2 Cinnamon Row, London SW11
Provides brochures on the US Virgin Islands.

BOOKS ABOUT THE CARIBBEAN
- *The Caribbean and its People*, T W Mayer, Wayland 1994 (age 11+)
- *Discovering Jamaica*, Alison Hodge, Zoë Books 1998 (age 11+)
- *World Focus: Jamaica*, John Barraclough, Heinemann 1995 (age 10+)

GLOSSARY

BAUXITE
The ore from which alumina is extracted, to manufacture aluminium.

COSMOPOLITAN
A word used to describe a population that is a mixture of people and cultures from many different parts of the world.

COUP D'ÉTAT
A violent or illegal change in government.

DEFORESTATION
The clearance of trees by people, either to burn them as fuelwood or to use the land for a different purpose, such as farming.

FREE TRADE ZONES
Areas that offer financial incentives to attract businesses.

GROSS DOMESTIC PRODUCT (GDP)
A similar measure to GNP, except that GDP does not include money earned by a country from investments abroad.

GROSS NATIONAL PRODUCT (GNP) PER CAPITA
The total value of all the goods and services produced by a country in a year, divided by the number of people in the country.

HYDRO-ELECTRICITY
Electricity produced by flowing water that drives a generator.

INDENTURED LABOURERS
People who agreed to work for several years at a set wage in return for their fare.

INTERCROPPING
Growing different crops together, in an irregular pattern, to use the land efficiently.

MULTINATIONALS
Companies operating in several countries. They are normally based in North America, Europe and Japan.

SALT PAN
A shallow lake of sea water that evaporates to leave salt.

SUBSISTENCE FARMING
Farming that only produces enough food for the family, with little or no surplus produce to sell.

TRANS-SHIPMENT PORTS
Major ports where goods are transferred from ships used in local trade to and from larger ocean-going container ships.

TROPICAL KARST
Limestone eroded by underground rivers that collapses and looks like eggboxes.

TROPICS
The latitudinal region lying between 23.5°N (the Tropic of Cancer) and 23.5°S (the Tropic of Capricorn) of the Equator 0°.